I0154509

MAGIC AND MEDICINE OF THE AZORES ISLANDS

Revised Edition

Jennifer Teixeira

ISBN 979-8-9855266-5-3

CONTENTS

INTRODUCTION

The Azores islands are a fascinating group of islands located in the Atlantic Ocean, with evidence of human habitation dating back to the 1500s. As an autonomous region of Portugal and part of the Macaronesian islands, the Azores offer a unique blend of culture and history. The climate is humid and temperate, influenced by the surrounding ocean. My family hails from the islands of Pico and Terceira, which are part of the central group of 5 islands, but the Azores as a whole comprise of 9 major islands. Interestingly, they are 850 miles west of continental Portugal and 2,400 miles from Boston, Massachusetts.

The 1960s was a tumultuous time in many parts of the world, and it was no different in the country of my grandparents. Civil unrest and lack of employment opportunities were rife, and the country was under the grip of a dictatorship. In the face of these challenges, my grandparents decided to uproot their entire families and relocate to California, searching for a better life. Amidst the few possessions they carried with them was a wooden mortar and pestle made of a found stone, which my grandmother treasured deeply. She used it to crush various herbs to create delicious sauces and soups, and it soon became an essential tool in her kitchen. The mortar and pestle was passed down to my mother, who also used it for many years until it became more of a relic than a functional kitchen tool. One day, this relic split in half, the cracks signaling the end of its usefulness. But the memories it held for my family will stay with us forever. The mortar and pestle represented the struggles and sacrifices of my grandparents, and the resourcefulness and resilience they displayed in the face of adversity. Today, when I think of the mortar and pestle, I am reminded of the importance of family traditions and the value of preserving heritage. It is a reminder always to cherish the things that matter, no matter how small or insignificant they may seem.

Growing up in a large Portuguese community in California, I had a unique upbringing compared to my parents. Despite being miles away from the land where we came from, there was always a strong love and connection to our roots. My parents always instilled in me an appreciation for our ancestry, and listening to their stories and visiting the villages they came from made me love my culture even more. One thing that particularly stood out to me was the emphasis on food as medicine. My family always believed every nutrient was useful in improving health for yourself and your loved ones. There was a special emphasis on digestive health, which was a major problem in the Azores during my parents' time. Access to healthy food (and sometimes any food at all) was difficult for many people, and so my family always made sure to eat nutritious meals to avoid any digestive issues.

Thankfully, times have changed in the Azores and there is much less poverty than there was even 20 years ago. After having lived in the United States for over 30 years, and after retiring, both my parents bought a house in Terceira and moved back for half the year. It's wonderful to see them reconnecting with their roots and experiencing the beauty of the land where they came from. Their love for our culture and heritage has only inspired me to continue learning more about my ancestry.

The study of folk medicine can be a challenging subject, especially when it comes to finding reliable sources of information. It requires extensive research and investigation to identify centenarians or individuals who have learned directly from them. However, this task is necessary to preserve valuable knowledge that may otherwise be lost forever, particularly in communities with high illiteracy rates that did not document their recipes and remedies. As someone who shares traditional herbalism from the Azores, I believe it is important to remember that if you plan to use herbs for healing, some of the best herbs are those grown around you. This perspective is rooted in folk herbalism, which emphasizes the healing potential of plants as they relate to a particular region and historical context. In my own exploration of the uses of herbs and culture, I've found a handful of plants and their uses that I hope to expand on further during my next visit. It's worth noting that some of us may already have these plants in our homes in the USA, Portugal, or elsewhere, without knowing how they benefit the people they travel with. This is why I feel it is important to share the history of plants and people, as it helps us understand how certain plants have been used over time to promote health and well-being. To me, this work is personal. My great-great-grandmother Deolinda was a midwife who helped bring my father into the world, making her the first person to hold him. When she passed away, my father was the last person to hold her hand and was with her until the end. On my matrilineal side, my great-grandmother Adelgiza had 13 children, 11 of whom survived to adulthood. Their experiences and knowledge have been passed down through the generations, and it is my hope that this information can be shared with a wider audience to continue the legacy of folk medicine.

Exploring the world of herbalism and folk magic of plants can be a challenging yet fascinating journey. Often, the plants used in folk medicine and remedies do not have scientific names or are mislabeled, making it difficult to remember and match them with their English names. Instead, these plants have been passed down through generations with their healing properties and uses being the focus rather than their names. Despite these challenges, there are some herbs that stand out and are commonly used in herbalism and folk magic. Garlic, for example, is a popular ingredient in many remedies due to its medicinal properties and versatility as a food. When exploring the world of herbalism and folk magic, it is essential to keep an open mind and be willing to learn about the different plants and their uses. For those who are interested in herbalism and folk magic, it can be helpful to cross-reference plants with images to ensure that the right plant is being used. This is especially true for those from a family with traditional practices and remedies, such as those in the Azores. By keeping an open mind and being willing to learn, one can discover the many benefits of herbalism and folk magic in everyday life.

REMEDIES

Onion, *Allium Cepa*, Cebola

Plants have been used for medicinal purposes for thousands of years, and onion is one such plant that has various health benefits. Onion, scientifically known as Allium cepa or Cebola, is a common kitchen ingredient that possesses anti-inflammatory, anti-bacterial, and antioxidant properties. One of the ways my mother used onion was by making onion peel tea, which was an excellent remedy for colds and coughs. The tea was made by boiling onion peels in water, and before you drank it, you would inhale the vapor to help open up your airways. This practice was particularly helpful, especially during the winter season when respiratory infections were common. To make the tea more palatable, my mother would add a little bit of honey, if available. However, for kids who did not like the taste of honey, beet sugar was used as an alternative. This method worked well to give the tea a pleasant taste that children could enjoy. Alternatively, onion peels could be used to make broths mixed with other vegetables that you had on hand, creating a hearty and nutritious soup. This was a great way to utilize onion peels and reduce food waste while also providing a delicious and healthy meal for the family. Overall, using onion for medicinal purposes is an excellent example of how simple kitchen ingredients can enhance our health and well-being.

Garlic, *Allium Sativum*, Alho

Garlic has been known for its delicious flavor and various health benefits. It is considered to be a protective food that can be found in almost every savory dish. However, not many people know that garlic can also be used topically to alleviate certain health problems. For instance, if you have an earache, you can crush garlic and mix it with olive oil. Then, apply the mixture to your ear and place a warm pack over it. This can help relieve the pain and discomfort associated with earaches. In addition, garlic can also be used to open up airways and prevent infections. To make a garlic and vinegar remedy, you would need to crush garlic and let it soak in vinegar for three or more days. Then, you can take a teaspoon of the liquid by mouth as needed. Some people prefer to mix the liquid with hot water and drink it like tea. Overall, garlic is a versatile ingredient that can be used in various ways to promote health and wellness. Whether you consume it in your food or use it topically, it can be an effective and natural way to treat certain ailments

Parsley, *Petroselinum Crispum*, Salsa

Parsley, with its distinctive fresh and slightly bitter flavor, is a very versatile herb that can be used in many dishes. It's one of those herbs that can be used in both cooked and raw forms, and it is considered an all-season herb. Parsley is also rich in vitamins A, C, and K, and minerals such as iron and calcium, which makes it a healthy addition to any dish. One traditional dish that uses parsley is a torta. To make it, you mix a generous amount of chopped parsley and crushed garlic with eggs and fry them. It's a simple yet delicious dish that can provide you with food for the whole day. Parsley is also a common ingredient in sauces, and one such sauce is "Môlho crú." It's made by crushing raw parsley and garlic with vinegar, and it's often used as a condiment for fish and meats. The raw garlic in the sauce is known for its antimicrobial properties, and parsley is known to help with kidney, stomach, and gallbladder pains.

Fennel, *Foeniculum vulgare*, Funcho

Fennel, a perennial herb with yellow flowers and feathery leaves, has been used for centuries in various cultures for its medicinal and culinary properties. My grandfather, for example, would often take a thin stalk of fennel and chew on it while gardening to help freshen his breath. But aside from being a natural breath freshener, fennel has a wide range of health benefits. In traditional medicine, vapor of fennel is used to open the airways in flu and colds. The plant is crushed in the hands and inhaled, sometimes crushed and placed on the chest for better breathing. Decoction of the roots is used to decrease menstrual pains, while the flowers are used to help with liver problems. Tea made from the leaves is given to nursing mothers and babies to help lessen the incidence of colic. And decoction of the seeds and leaves is used for digestive issues. One interesting recipe that my cousin calls "hair soup" is actually just fennel soup. It's made using beans, pig knuckles or ham hocks, potatoes, and of course fennel. It was one way to get nutrition and help with respiratory and stomach aches, as well as lactation. It's worth noting, however, that fennel has been shown to increase estrogen levels, so use it with caution in estrogen-sensitive bodies. Overall, fennel is a versatile herb that can be used in many different ways. Whether you're looking to freshen your breath, ease menstrual pains, or aid digestion, fennel may be worth considering.

Loquat, *Eriobotrya japonica*, Nespera

Loquat is a small, sweet fruit that is native to China. It has found its way to the Azores where it grows plentifully. Interestingly, loquat has been associated with several health benefits, especially for expectant mothers. For instance, my grandmother would crave loquats when she was pregnant, and she believed that the fruit prevented the baby from being born with its mouth open. At first, I wasn't quite sure what this saying meant, so I decided to look into it further. I asked around and even did some online research. I thought it might mean a cleft palate or breathing problems, or even having a big mouth. However, I discovered that it was just slang for being born stupid, which was quite surprising. Despite the slang connotation, loquats are a great source of nutrition for expectant mothers. The fruit is high in Vitamin A and B-Vitamins, including Folate, which is essential for fetal development. In addition to its nutritional value, loquat is also known to help alleviate nausea, a common symptom of pregnancy. Overall, whether or not you believe in the old saying about loquats, there's no denying that this small fruit has a lot to offer. So, if you're an expectant mother or you just enjoy tasty, nutritious fruit, be sure to add some loquats to your diet.

Calamint, *Nepeta cater*, Neveda

Camphorous calamint, also known as Calamintha nepeta, is a herbaceous plant that grows in the Mediterranean region and is used for its numerous medicinal properties. When the leaves of this plant are crushed in the hand and inhaled, they can help to open up the airways, making it easier to breathe. Apart from this, calamint is also used to calm the nerves. It is made into an alcoholic drink and consumed to help soothe anxiety and promote relaxation. The leaves of the plant can also be smoked to help relieve tooth pain. Calamint is also known to be helpful for digestive stress. It can be made into an infusion that can be consumed to relieve symptoms such as bloating, indigestion, and flatulence. In fact, it is often recommended for children who are experiencing digestive discomfort as it is a gentle and effective remedy. I have a personal experience with Calamint as well. I remember my grandmother making a tea with it for me when I was sick with a cold as a child. The infusion helped to calm and relax me, making it easier for me to rest and recover. Overall, calamint is a versatile and valuable herb that has been used for centuries for its numerous health benefits.

Mallow, *Malva Sylvestris*, Malva

The common mallow plant is often overlooked and considered a weed by many people. However, this plant has many medicinal properties that have been used for generations. My grandmother would often use this plant to help heal wounds by crushing it into a paste and applying it to injuries such as scraped knees, cuts, and burns. She would also heat the mallow leaves and place them on skin infections for relief. The leaves of the common mallow plant are also useful for tired and sore feet. A hot infusion of the leaves can be made to soak in a footbath, providing a soothing and relaxing effect. The flowers of the plant can also be gathered to make tea that can help with heartburn and other gastrointestinal issues. The amount of flowers used would depend on the severity of the situation. It's fascinating how useful this plant can be when utilized correctly. Despite its medicinal properties, this plant is often disregarded by many individuals. It just goes to show that sometimes the most overlooked things can have the most significant benefits.

Rosemary, *Rosmarinus officinalis*, Alecrim

The history of rosemary is intertwined with the traditional uses of this plant. However, there are many stories of poverty and struggle, including the practice of leaving babies at "Casa de Roda". These places were usually run by nuns and provided a way for parents to leave unplanned babies under complete anonymity. The nunnery was built like a church/fortress, which is a testament to the poverty and pillaging of resources during those times, due to the presence of pirates. The term "Casa de Roda" translates to "Wheel House". The child would be surrendered to the chamber of the wheel, and it would be turned to pass to the nuns on the other side, ensuring complete anonymity. Food and supplies were also delivered in this way, so men and nuns could not lay eyes on each other. Now, you may be wondering what all of this has to do with rosemary. Well, here's where it gets interesting. Fresh or dried rosemary was used to induce abortion when given strong doses of tea for a week straight. This practice was also reported with parsley and chamomile, which goes to show that even herbs we think of as gentle can have unexpected responses when taken in large doses. As the saying goes, "sola dosis facit venenum". It's important to note that women were responsible for much of the heavy lifting when it came to raising a family. It was not uncommon in the Catholic Society of the time to have ten or more children 50 years ago. Despite all the hardships, the traditional uses of plants such as rosemary have been passed down through generations and provide us with a glimpse into the past.

Rue, *Ruta Chalepensis*, Arruda

Rue has significant cultural and historical significance in the Azores. The plant is used medicinally to remove the "evil eye," a common belief in many cultures. The "evil eye" is thought to cause all kinds of diseases and is usually due to jealousy and covetousness of others. My grandmother, who was from the Azores, loved to drink Rue leaf tea and used Rue to ward against evil. Rue is commonly used for this purpose in Mediterranean regions, and this folk medicine traveled to the Azores as well. According to tradition, a cup of the brew left overnight would remove negative influences from the house and the people living in it. The tea was then thrown out of the front door, and Rue was planted by the doorway to prevent people with negative intent from entering. Rue was also used internally as tea in folk remedies for kidney and bladder pain. My grandmother believed that drinking Rue tea would remove "evil" from the body. She also used it as a mouthwash for tooth pain and to improve her vision as an eyewash.

Lantana, *Lantana Camara*, Camarat

Lantana is a beautiful flowering plant that is native to tropical America, but it has since spread to various parts of the world. While it is often admired for its vibrant colors and sweet fragrance, it is important to note that it is also an invasive plant that can cause harm to humans and animals. However, despite its potential dangers, Lantana has been used for medicinal purposes for centuries. One of the most popular uses of Lantana is to make syrup that can help soothe throats and coughs. In fact, my Tia (aunt) used to pick the flowers and leaves of the Lantana that were growing by the sea, specifically at remnants of a tuff volcano called Monte Brasil on Terceira Island, and she would dry them to make a cough syrup. The syrup made from Lantana is known to have anti-inflammatory and antibacterial properties that can help alleviate coughs and colds. In addition to its medicinal properties, Lantana is also used for decorative purposes. During holy festivals, people often use Lantana flowers to decorate the streets. The vibrant colors and sweet fragrance of Lantana flowers make them a popular choice for decorating religious processions and holy sites. However, it is important to note that not all parts of the Lantana plant are safe for consumption. The unripe berries of the plant are considered toxic to humans and can cause liver damage. In addition, the plant is toxic to livestock and can cause harm to animals. As such, it is important to exercise caution when using Lantana for medicinal or decorative purposes. Overall, Lantana is a fascinating and versatile plant that has been used for centuries for various purposes. While its invasive nature and potential dangers cannot be ignored, its medicinal and decorative properties are certainly noteworthy

Carrot, *Daucus carota var.*, Cenoura.

Carrot syrup is a traditional recipe that has been passed down through generations. One of the recipes that I came across was the raw carrot syrup. It is a simple recipe that can be made with just two ingredients - carrot root and beet sugar. It is believed to help ease a sore throat, which makes it an ideal home remedy during the cold and flu season. To make this syrup, you will need to slice the carrot root very thin and layer it with beet sugar. It is recommended to use beet sugar as it was more common in the Azores, where this recipe originates, than cane sugar, but you can use white cane sugar as well. After layering the carrots and sugar, let it sit for two days. During this time, the carrots will dry up, and the sugar will become syrupy. Once the two days are up, strain the syrup and store it in a clean bottle or jar. You can take a spoonful of this syrup whenever you have a sore throat or cough. Not only is it an effective remedy, but it is also a delicious and healthy way to consume carrots. So, the next time you're feeling under the weather, try making this raw carrot syrup. It's a simple, natural, and effective way to soothe a sore throat.

Spearmint, *Mentha spicata,* hortelã

After giving birth, it is traditional for women to rest for nine days. During this time, they are taken care of and given special foods to help with their recovery. One of these foods is Canja, a delicious chicken soup with rice. Canja is made in different ways depending on the family, but it typically includes broth, garlic, onion, chicken, and rice with a little bit of carrot chopped up into small pieces. What sets Canja apart is the addition of spearmint, which is added fresh after the soup has cooked to help with digestion and offer a cooling, anti-inflammatory effect. The garlic and onions in the soup are believed to help combat any infections in the body that may have arisen from the delivery process. Meanwhile, the chicken and rice offer protein and carbohydrates to help with the exhaustion new mothers often feel after giving birth. Spearmint is also added to Sopas as a garnish and as a refreshing tea to drink after meals. Its digestive properties are not only enjoyable but also helpful in aiding the body's recovery process.

Coffee Senna, *Senna occidentalis,* Fedegoso

I wanted to share a story with you about my cousin who helped an aging woman whose hair kept falling out of her head. It was a distressing situation for the woman, but my cousin knew just what to do. She gave this woman a tea of Fedegoso to drink and to apply onto her scalp to help her hair come back. To everyone's amazement, fedegoso worked in this case! Without knowing for sure why the woman's hair was falling out, I can't tell you how it worked, but fedegoso is used as a potent antifungal, antiparasitic, detoxifying herb that can decrease inflammation and boost immunity. It is quite remarkable how certain herbs can have such a profound effect on our health and well-being.

Hydrangea, *Hydrangea macrophylla* Hortência

The hydrangea, a plentiful invasive plant, is a common sight on the Azores islands. In fact, its growth is so abundant that the Azores are often referred to as the "Purple Islands." The hydrangea's beautiful flowers, which range in color from light lavender to deep purple, are used to decorate the streets during the procession of the saints, in churches, and on archways. Despite its invasive nature, the hydrangea has become a beloved plant in the Azores and can be found growing everywhere on the islands. It's not just the flowers that have practical uses. Dried roots of the plant are crushed and mixed with warm oil to create a topical treatment for arthritic pain. However, it's important to note that picking the hydrangea flowers from the roadside or in parks is illegal. While they may be beautiful and tempting, it's crucial to allow these plants to thrive and continue to contribute to the lush landscape of the Azores.

White Horehound, *Marrubium vulgare*, Marroio

White horehound tea is a popular and commonly used beverage in the Azores Islands. It has been used for centuries to treat respiratory complaints, including coughs, colds, and bronchitis. But did you know that it can also be used as a natural remedy to lower blood sugar levels in people with type 2 diabetes? White horehound is a herbaceous plant that belongs to the mint family. It is native to Europe, Asia, and North Africa and has been cultivated for its medicinal properties for centuries. The plant contains several active compounds, including marrubiin, which has been shown to have hypoglycemic effects. Several studies have suggested that white horehound tea can help lower blood sugar levels in people with type 2 diabetes. One study published in the Journal of Ethnopharmacology found that white horehound tea significantly reduced blood glucose levels in diabetic rats. Another study published in the Journal of Herbal Medicine showed that drinking white horehound tea for 12 weeks significantly reduced fasting blood glucose levels in people with type 2 diabetes.

Saint John's Wort *Hypericum perforatum*, hipericão

One of the most popular festivals related to this plant is the Festival of Saint John, (San Joaninas) which is celebrated on June 21st. This date coincides with the Summer Solstice, which is believed to be a time of great power and energy. During the Festival of Saint John, people gather bundles of herbs and flowers, including the small St. John's Wort. These flowers are known to have medicinal properties and can be used to help with nerve complaints when made into a poultice. They are also considered a symbol of good luck and protection. Throughout history, the Festival of Saint John has been associated with various pagan practices gradually assimilating into Christianity. The celebration of fertility, the burning of evil spirits, and the creation of bonfires are just some of the traditions that have been passed down through generations. These days, the festival is celebrated in Portugal and other parts of the world. In some countries, it is known as the Midsummer Festival, and it is celebrated with similar traditions. Flowers of all colors line the streets, and people light bonfires at midnight. Participants jump over the flames to burn away evil and for protection. Overall, the Festival of Saint John is a celebration of nature, fertility, and the power of the sun. It is a time to gather with friends and family, share food and drink, and honor the traditions of our ancestors. Whether you believe in the medicinal properties of St. John's Wort or not, there is no denying the beauty and symbolism associated with this plant.

Grape, *Vitis vinifera* Uvas

Grapes are one of the most popular fruits in the world, and they are used for a variety of purposes. They are not only a delicious snack, but they are also packed with nutrients and have a number of health benefits. One of the most commonly known benefits of grapes is that they can help prevent constipation. This is because they are high in fiber, which helps to regulate bowel movements and keep your digestive system healthy. In addition to their health benefits, grapes are also used to make a variety of products, including wine. Wine has been a popular drink for centuries, and it is enjoyed by people all over the world. In the Azores islands, wine is considered a wonderful offering to the land and ancestors. The volcanic soil of the Azores islands gives the grapes a unique flavor, which is reflected in the wine produced there.

Tea, *Camelia Sinensis*, chá

Black tea was used medicinally in the Azores to help postpartum mothers after birthing their child. A specific type of black tea, known as Cha Gorreana Preto, was given to mothers after delivery to help with milk production and provide energy via caffeine content. It was also believed to help move the bowels and get things flowing, which is essential for postpartum mothers. Although I did not have the opportunity to try this after delivering my child, a Tia who has given birth to babies claimed that this was what helped, especially when combined with milk. Adding milk would not only enhance the taste of the tea but also provide additional nutrients for the mother and baby. It's fascinating to think that something as simple as a cup of tea could profoundly impact a person's health.

Seaweed, *Porphyra sp., Ulva rigida, Osmundea pinnatifida, and Fucus Spiralis*, Ervhas Du Calhao~

Seaweed has been a significant part of the Azorean diet for centuries. It was once considered a staple food source for the locals, and many people made a living by harvesting it. My Tio was one of them. As a young man, he would go diving and harvesting seaweed off rocks for sale. Although he may not have known the scientific names of the different types of seaweed, he chose them according to what

23

people were eating at the time. Sadly, seaweed is not as commonly used in food anymore, as it was considered "poor man's food." However, it is making a comeback due to the Azorean people's renewed interest in healthy and local food. Seaweed is a nutrient-dense food that contains vitamins, minerals, antioxidants, and fiber, making it an excellent addition to a healthy diet. One type of seaweed that is commonly found in the Azores is Fucus Spiralis. This species of seaweed has a bit of seasonal variability, with protein and carbohydrates being higher in a winter harvest, while lipids and fiber are higher in a summer harvest. Fucus Spiralis is commonly used in soups, stews, and other traditional Azorean dishes. It's fascinating to see how the food culture in the Azores has evolved over time. While some traditional foods have been forgotten, others are being rediscovered and appreciated for their nutritional value and unique flavors.

Here is a recipe originally from Corvo Island ~ "Tortas du Ervas Du Calhao"
Ingredients:
Handful of fresh "Ervas Du Calhao" chopped
1 small chopped onion
6 cloves of garlic crushed
Teaspoon Piri Piri or other crushed pepper sauce
5 eggs
Sometimes you can add a little bit of flour (tablespoon) if you have it.

Mix all of this together in a bowl, and then fry in olive oil like you would pancakes.

Another way to use the seaweed was to cover it with vinegar to use later on with some of the seawater. Essentially a pickled seaweed.

Portuguese Broom *Cytisus striatus*

On May 1st, the festival of Os Maios is celebrated in the Azores and the rest of Portugal. This festival includes gathering Portuguese Broom, which is then used to clean the home and freshen the air. The Brooms are made of a plant that is commonly called "Portuguese Broom". The tradition goes that these brooms are hung over the doorway from April 30th to May 1st to bless and protect the house. The festival is also known for the creation of life-sized dolls, which are created and stuffed, traditionally with Rye, but this has changed over the years. These dolls create the illusion of people doing work, while the participants of the festival enjoy food and drink wine. The festival is a celebration of spring and the renewal of life, as well as a time to give thanks for the blessings of the previous year. The festival is a wonderful way to experience Portuguese culture and traditions, and it is an event that is not to be missed if you ever find yourself in Portugal during the month of May.

Japanese silverberry, *Elaeagnus Umbellata*, Bagueira: Or by the name I knew it as growing up: "Groselha"

As a child I would pucker at the sour and astringent flavor of the tiny berries on this plant. They are about the size of a currant, and lightly spotted silvery white (Where I imagine it gets its name) We would call it "Groselha" , which translates to "Currants" though it is not a currant, it is commonly referred to as Groselha in the Azores. It is in the family Elaeagnaceae (oleaster family) and currants are of a different grouping.   I remember my father stating loudly that the plant grew so fast, he had a hard time keeping the shrub trimmed so that it did not take over our small yard. The flowers came on with a sweet smell and inviting energy, though the shrub was protected by small thorns on its branches . The berries take patience to pick, when we made syrups from them, it was a time consuming process of our little hands gently plucking each berry off individually and being sure to remove the stem. Each berry held onto one seed surrounded by tart fruit that the birds loved to eat and help with its propagation. Initially my father planted it along with a fig tree to help with the growth of the fig and because it was a favorite fruit of his childhood. Japanese Silverberry has been shown to enrich the soil around it, and increase production of fruit trees near it. This is a small invasive tree or bush introduced to the Azores from Asia. The berry of this plant is highly astringent and is full of vitamin C, A, E, carotenoids, has EFAs and is higher in lycopene than tomatoes. The leaves can be used to help stop diarrhea when made into an infusion while A syrup similar to Grenadine is made with the berries to flavor drinks and increase vitamin C levels in the seafaring people. The branches and leaves of this plant are also used to make brooms.

Groselha Syrup:

4 cups silverberries

4 cups water

2 cups honey (approx)

Simmer the berries and water for an hour or so while stirring and crushing them in the pan. Once you feel like the juice has been fully expressed, you can strain the pulp and seed out to set aside for another project, or compost. Add equal amounts of honey to liquid and stir well. Alternatively you can cover the berries in aguardente (it encourages sailors to drink it!) and crush them without heat and add beet sugar or honey later on; though simmering the berries in water greatly increases the lycopene content.

Firetree, *Morella Faia,* Myrica Faia

The Firetree, also known as Myrica Faya, is a fascinating native tree that is found in Macaronesia. It is a dioecious plant, which means that it has male and female flowers on separate trees. This fast-growing tree was used by the Azorean people for various purposes such as making brooms, wine, and medicine. The brooms made with Faya were used to sweep out ash in the wood-burning ovens. The wood from this tree was also used to heat the fires of these ovens. The Myrica Faya is part of the Myricaceae family of plants and has a curly-leafed appearance, similar to that of a bay tree. The tree produces either seeds or blackberry-looking fruits, and the berries are used to make wine, while the seeds are used to make medicine. Interestingly, there is even a musical band named after this plant on Terceira island, which is very popular. However, the Myrica Faya has also become an invasive species in places like Hawaii, where it changes the nitrogen level in soils, making it inhabitable to native Hawaiian plants. Apart from its various uses, the Firetree Morella Faia also has medicinal properties. The leaves of this tree are used to help with hair growth and are simmered (decocted), cooled, and applied to the scalp. A poultice of the burnt seeds mixed with oil or fat is used topically to treat wounds and as an analgesic.

Tia Maria gave me this recipe of a remedy to help with lactation and to build strength after labor :

Caldo de Ovo (Egg Soup)
2 eggs
1 tbsp vinegar
1 tsp cumin, *Cuminum cyminum,* aduvos)
Sea salt
Lard
You would beat it all together in a bowl and then pour boiling water over it slowly, stirring so as not to curdle. Bread was added, and then was eaten like a

thick soup.

Soup is one of my favorite foods, there is so much variety to it, and so many possibilities. You can create a broth with simple ingredients, letting nothing go to waste or be as extravagant as you want. Onion peels, carrot tops and bones make excellent broths. Great for elders and young people alike. There is a delicate balance between making something delicious and healthy. Using top quality ingredients is key in anything you make.

My mother had been a caretaker of my aunts and uncle since she was 5 years old. Both of her parents worked more than full time in the Azores. She was expected to take care of the children, and provide food for them, even if there was not much available. She perfected the "Poor Man's Soup" Caldo Verde. Caldo Verde simply translates to "green soup". Since collards are plentiful in the Azores a generous amount of collards will turn the soup green, this is the traditional Caldo Verde. The leaves are cut into thin strips and the mashed potatoes are used to help thicken the soup. I love when my mom cooks for me, and I have adapted her recipe to my environment now so I can enjoy it in my home.

Since I have nettles and comfrey growing plentifully in the spring, I like to make

This is Caldo Verde with foraged herbs and homegrown vegetables. When I have more collards growing, I will also make it the traditional way.

Ingredients:

1 cup fresh harvested and boiled nettle leaf cut into

strips.
3 hands length young fresh leaves of comfrey cut into thin strips
2-3 medium sized potatoes peeled and quartered
3 cloves crushed garlic
3 stems of 3 cornered leeks chopped.
4 cups of water, nettle tea or *broth
Tablespoon olive oil or fat
Splash of white wine (optional)
Linguica or sausage disks (optional)

Add your olive oil to a small soup pot and turn to medium heat. Add your chopped leeks and garlic to the pot to simmer for about a minute. You can add a splash of white wine if you want, then add the potatoes and water or broth to cover. Let it simmer till the potatoes are cooked, then you can use a stick blender, sieve or fork to mash the potatoes and garlic. Add your nettles and comfrey to simmer for 10 minutes. Add sea salt or dulse to taste. * You can use the leftover water from cooking the nettles to use in the soup if you want, or I like to use bone broth that I make in advance and have on hand in the freezer or canning jars. I give the nettle water to my chickens.

Sopa de Funcho (hair soup)

1 ½ cup dry pinto beans (or what you like)
2 smoked ham hocks
2 bulbs of fennel with leaves
1 medium onion chopped
10 cloves of garlic crushed and chopped
3 cups cubed potatoes

Splash of white wine.
Bay leaf
8 cups water or broth
Salt and pepper to taste
Olive oil approx 3 tablespoons

Cook Your beans.

In a 4 Qt soup pot, fry the onion in the olive oil till translucent, then add the garlic. Chop the Funcho (fennel and leaves) Chiffonade. Add in a splash of white wine to the onions and garlic, then Add 8 cups of water or broth, add your ham hocks, potatoes, and cooked beans. Let them cook until soft, for about one hour. Then you can add the rest of the ingredients and simmer on medium heat for 20 minutes. The people in the Azores will add Linguica to everything, if it is available, so feel free to add that to the pot towards the end if it is something you want.

Canja de Galinha
This is a comforting soup that I love to make on rainy days. It is also best known as an easy to make gentle soup for people recovering from illness both physical and emotional.
Ingredients:

1 medium onion
1 clove garlic
12 cups Broth (made with chicken fat, bay leaves, ginger and whatever else you have on hand that you like.)
½ - 1 cup rice (1 cup if you like it thick)
Chicken thigh chopped into small bits

1 chopped potato
1 chopped carrot
1 teaspoon dried seaweed of choice.
2 tablespoons olive oil

In a hot pot simmer the chopped onion, garlic, and carrot first. Add seaweed then potatoes and stir. Put in enough broth to cook these ingredients until soft. Use an immersion blender, blender or masher to puree. Then add the rest of the broth, chopped chicken and rice. Stir and simmer for 2 minutes, then when the pot is boiling do one final stir and cover while you turn off the heat. In 20 minutes come back and give it a stir. Add some piri piri or hot sauce (if you like) to the bowl and enjoy.

HISTORY OF PORTUGAL AND ANCIENT RELIGIONS

Viriato led the Lusitanians; at about 200 BC, the Romans defeated the Carthaginians that had occupied what is now known as Northern Portugal; the Lusitanians were not as friendly or easy to conquer; they held off the Romans in many legendary battles; Viriato, the Lusitanian leader had been successful until the Romans bribed a trusted Lusitanian Official to kill Viriato. This led to the fall of the Lusitanians to Roman power.

This is just one of the many pagan influences you will see in the history of the Azores; as time has passed, religions have changed, and we are beginning to see a resurgence of people looking into the spiritual practices of their most ancient ancestors. The Proto Celtic tribe of Lusitanians had their main deities of worship.

Some Lusitanian Goddesses And Gods:

Endovelicus

Health, Prosperity, Life *Santuário da Rocha da Mina* (Mina's Rock Sanctuary) in Southern Portugal is said to be a temple to Endovelicus; not far from this place, there is a sacred and much older fountain said to have healing properties. You will see "EX

IMPERATO AVERNO" at the site, which suggests this was where one would seek oracles. It roughly translates to "From what emanated from below." Endovelicus was a God of Healing, one of the Underworld, and had Chthonic attributes. Romans Equated Endovelicus to Asclepis and Greco-Roman Sarapis

Ataegina

The Goddess of Dawn, was an important deity in ancient Gaulish and Iberian religions. She was called upon for a variety of reasons, including protection of the home and the family, as well as for cursing enemies. She was also known as the Goddess of life, death, and rebirth, and was associated with the agricultural cycles of birth, growth, and decay. In the Roman pantheon, Ataegina was often equated with Proserpina, or the Greek goddess Persephone. Like these goddesses, Ataegina was associated with the underworld and the cycle of life and death. She was also linked to the moon and the night, and was sometimes invoked in rituals of divination and magic. The goat was a sacred animal of Ataegina, and was often depicted in her images and sculptures. This animal was associated with fertility, abundance, and vitality, and was considered a symbol of the goddess's power and protection. Ataegina was usually mentioned with three epithets: Domina, Sancta, and Turibri(gae). These titles emphasized her power and authority, as well as her connection to the natural world. The

Goddess of Dawn was seen as a force of nature, representing the power of the sun to bring life and light to the world. And her role as a protector of the home and family made her an important figure in the daily lives of the people who worshipped her.

The Goddess Nabia

Also known as Nábia or Nabiça, was a deity worshipped in ancient times by the Lusitanian people, who inhabited what is now Portugal. She was considered the goddess of valleys and rivers, and was believed to have the power to control the waters and the fertility of the land. One of the most important places of worship dedicated to Nabia was the Fountain of the Idol, located in Continental Portugal. This sacred spot was believed to be a portal between the mortal world and the divine realm, where the goddess could be contacted and her blessings and favors could be obtained. The Fountain of the Idol is a beautiful and serene place, surrounded by lush vegetation and the sound of flowing water. It is said that the water from the fountain has healing properties, and that it can bring good luck and prosperity to those who drink from it. Today, the legacy of Nabia can still be felt in the traditions and folklore of Portugal. Many people still visit the Fountain of the Idol to pay homage to this ancient goddess and to connect with the natural world around them. The Goddess Nabia may no longer be worshipped as she once was, but her spirit lives on in the hearts of those who appreciate the beauty and power of nature.

Epona

In ancient Portugal, the Goddess Epona was a revered deity known for her protective and nurturing nature. She was particularly associated with the well-being of horses and donkeys, and was believed to watch over the safety and prosperity of all those who worked with these animals. Her name was invoked in times of need by farmers, herdsmen, and travelers alike, who sought her blessing and guidance on their journeys. Today, Epona remains a symbol of strength, grace, and compassion, reminding us of the enduring bond between humans and the animals we share our world with.

Trebaruna:

In ancient Portugal, the Goddess Trebaruna was widely worshiped as the deity of war. Her Roman equivalent was Victoria, with her name possibly meaning "House" and "Mystery". She was the patron goddess of warriors, and many soldiers would seek her guidance and protection before going into battle. It was believed that her divine power could help them emerge victorious in even the most challenging of conflicts. Apart from her association with war and victory, Trebaruna was also revered for her mysterious and enigmatic nature. Her name itself suggests a connection to the concept of "mystery" and "house", which only adds to the intrigue and mystique surrounding her. Despite being a powerful and revered goddess, much about Trebaruna remains shrouded in mystery and is yet to be fully understood by modern scholars. Nevertheless, her legacy lives on, and her influence can still be felt in modern-day Portugal. Many people continue to pay homage to this ancient deity, seeking her blessings and guidance in their personal and professional lives. For those who believe in her power, Trebaruna remains a symbol of strength, courage, and victory - a true goddess of war.

The Goddess Bandua

Known as the deity of thermal waters and fords in Portuguese mythology, Bandua is often invoked for protection during travel over water. According to legend, she presides over the protective waters that guard those who journey across rivers and seas, and her divine influence is said to bring safety and good fortune to those who seek her aid. In ancient times, Bandua was worshipped by the people of Portugal as a powerful and benevolent goddess who could harness the mystical powers of the natural world. It was believed that she had the ability to control the flow of water and turn it into a protective barrier against danger, especially when it came to crossing rivers and other bodies of water. As a symbol of her power and influence, Bandua was often depicted in artwork and sculptures as a beautiful woman with long flowing hair, holding a staff or wand that represented her control over the elements. She was also sometimes shown with a serpent coiled around her arm, which was said to be a symbol of her healing and transformative abilities. Today, the worship of Bandua is still practiced by some people in Portugal who believe in her power to protect and guide them on their journeys. Whether you are embarking on a long voyage or simply navigating the challenges of everyday life, the spirit of Bandua can provide comfort and inspiration on your path.

The Holy Ghost

The archipelago of the Azores has its unique traditions and practices that are deeply rooted in its history, religion, and way of life. One of the most notable cultural practices in the Azores is the "Culto do Divino Espírito Santo" or the "Cult of the Holy Ghost" in English. The "Cult of the Holy Ghost" is a religious and cultural celebration that originated in the Azores in the 16th century. It is a manifestation of the Catholic faith, which has been the dominant religion in the Azores since the Portuguese colonization. The celebration is held annually in many towns and villages throughout the archipelago, with each community having its unique traditions and customs. During the "Cult of the Holy Ghost" celebration, a group of people is chosen to represent the Holy Spirit and its attributes. These people dress up and go from door to door, singing and collecting offerings. The offerings are used to fund a feast that is held later in the day, where everyone in the community is invited to partake in a meal that includes traditional dishes and delicacies. The "Cult of the Holy Ghost" celebration is not limited to the religious aspects of the festivity. It is also a time for families, friends, and neighbors to come together and strengthen their bonds. For many Azoreans, the "Cult of the Holy Ghost" celebration is a time to reconnect with their roots, honor their ancestors, and celebrate their cultural heritage. So, if you ever find yourself in the Azores during the "Cult of the Holy Ghost" celebration, be sure to join in on the festivities. It is an excellent opportunity to experience the Azorean culture at its finest and witness the living, breathing history of this unique archipelago.

Culture

There are significant religious rituals and ceremonies that can help one connect to the origins of these energies. In mid-February or the beginning of March, the Entrudo or Carnaval, also known as "Farewell to Flesh," is celebrated as a preparation for Easter. This event includes food, dance festivities, and artistic expressions like comedic performances, drag shows, and "Matrofonas." The American equivalent of this festival is Mardi Gras or Fat Tuesday. It is a time of excess, in preparation for the "Farewell to Flesh" on Good Friday.

On May 1st, Os Maios is celebrated, which involves gathering of Portuguese Broom to clean the home and freshen the air. Brooms made of a plant known as "Portuguese Broom" are hung over the doorway from April 30 to May 1st to bless and protect the house. Life-sized dolls are created and stuffed with rye or other materials to create the look of activity and work.

June 21st marks the Festival of Saint John, also known as "Sanjoaninas." Celebrated for generations before Catholicism became the law of the land, this festival marks the Summer Solstice. During this time, pagan rituals were performed to celebrate fertility, including gathering of bundles of herbs and flowers, including the small yellow flower "Saint John's Wort," which blossoms around this time and is said to bless the home and person gathering it. Flowers of all colors are used to line the streets and create beautiful decorations, and locals still take great pride in the colorful and cheery displays that can be seen throughout the summer months. The festival is reminiscent of pagan traditions of the Summer Solstice. Bonfires are created and lit at midnight, and participants jump over the flames to burn away evil and be protected. The festival of Saint John is celebrated on several islands of the Azores and in several cities across continental Portugal.

As you visit the Azores islands, you will notice a trend, places are named after the rocks and stones that they resemble. There are places named after such images, like Cachorro (little dog) in Pico island and Circle of Bear in Terceira Island. One of my favorite visions is the story of the Tuff Volcano known as Mount Brasil. As a woman and a priestess, I think of the places where the goddess hides, and I create my own magical journeys through each place of magnetic power. If you ask for visions of the Goddess in the Azores Islands, you will start seeing a few things. Above the City of Angra Do Heroismo, high on the hill overlooking the ocean, you will see the image of Mount Brasil. There, you will envision the story of the woman who gave birth to the sea and all of the oceanic creatures and people who lived near her waters. She is often compared to the Yoruban Yemaya, a Goddess of Creation, of mountains rising up from the sea, and the Mother of Fishes. Pay attention to the belly of the Volcano, reaching up to the sky, pregnant and full, ready to erupt as her legs spread out and toward the ocean, releasing the contents of her womb, populating the sea with her children and providing food for all. Sometimes, she reminds onlookers of the Volcanic Polynesian Madame Pele, and we are reminded that it is the Divine Feminine that gives birth to all life and just as easily she can be a destroyer of life. Her duality in death and life is the divine influence we feel with everything that we do in this world. This image reminds everyone of their own mother, the womb with which they are born through. It is symbolic of your own eruption into the world, and the explosion of stars that first propelled your essence into being. Within Mount Brasil, deep in the mountain, there is said to be a hidden temple, one of undetermined age and origin

Archaeologists from the Portuguese Association of Archaeological Research have discovered what they believe to be an ancient Carthaginian temple dedicated to the Goddess Tanit, dating back to the 4th century BC. The team has found more than five tombs carved into rocks and at least three proto-historic sanctuaries in the area. While there is some debate surrounding the validity of these findings, the structures are undoubtedly ancient. Tanit's Phoenician equivalent was believed to be Astarte, with both goddesses being associated with sailors. A statue of Tanit can be seen in the irrigation fountain of Jardim Duque Da Terceira. The alleged temple contains basins to collect liquid, and many of the tombs are shaped like a uterus, indicating that some form of sacrifice took place. Water appears to have held significant value in this area, as evidenced by the numerous public fountains. One of the temples is located near the ocean's waters, which was essential for creating a sanctuary in worship of ancient deities. A few structures are said to be similar to Roman Columbarium; the purpose being to hold the ashes of the dead. The Phoenicians settled in Spain around 600 BC, and the Mount Brazil area is considered a place of power on the island. It is also a site of death, with the Tuff Volcano being home to the Portuguese Military and the Castelo de

São João Baptista.

Hypogea on Terceira Island. (Image by author)

SUPERSTITIONS

The presence of the Roman Catholic Church in the Azores can be traced back to the island's earliest inhabitants. This is a common occurrence in regions that were conquered by the Roman Empire, and as a result, there is a Catholic church on every street in the Azores. However, this is not a comprehensive guide to the magic practices that can be found in these autonomous islands. To understand Azorean folk magic, we need to take into account the different cultural influences, including Portuguese, Mediterranean, African, Romani, and Seafarer traditions. Due to the dominance of Catholicism in the Azores, fueled by the Inquisitions and Crusades, there was a lot of fear surrounding witchcraft and magical activities. Many people who were accused of practicing magic had to flee to the Azores to avoid persecution. As someone with Azorean ancestry, I can provide insights into the magical practices that I have witnessed on the islands, as well as historical research. However, it's important to note that this is my own understanding and not a definitive guide to Azorean folk magic.

Pentacles

Pentacles as a good luck charm for children. These small objects are believed to protect kids from the evil eye and bring them good fortune. Pentacles are still widely used in the Azores as a way to bless and protect children. They are often given as gifts on special occasions such as baptisms, communions, and birthdays. Parents, grandparents, and other family members will attach the Pentacle to the child's clothing or jewelry so they can carry it with them wherever they go. The Pentacles themselves come in a variety of shapes and materials, but they all share the same basic design: a five-pointed star surrounded by a circle. Some Pentacles are made of silver or gold, while others are made of wood, ceramic, or other materials. The important thing is not the material, however, but the intention behind the gift.

Blessed Fabric

When a flag of the Holy Ghost/Santo Cristo or altar cloth from a church is no longer needed, it can be transformed into a lucky charm. You can simply place the fabric at the bottom of your purse for good luck while you're out of the house, or use it for extra protection during travel. Alternatively, you can create a small charm bag with the fabric. This piece of fabric can also be used in a similar way to a "Cartas Da Tocar" and can be blessed by a priest for good luck.

"Fig Hand"

The "Fig Hand" charm has been used for centuries as a symbol of good luck and protection against the evil eye. It is believed that this charm, when worn by children and adults, has the power to ward off negative energies and bring good fortune to the wearer. The charm is usually made of silver or gold and is shaped like a hand with fingers curled inward towards the palm. Interestingly, the "Fig Hand" charm is said to resemble the female anatomy, particularly the genitalia, which is why it is sometimes referred to as "Pussy". In certain cultures, the charm is associated with copulation and fecundity, representing the fertility and abundance that come with sexual union. Despite its suggestive appearance and associations, the "Fig Hand" charm is considered a powerful talisman that can bring good luck and protection to those who wear it. It is often given as a gift to friends and family members, or purchased for oneself as a symbol of personal power and protection. The "Fig Hand" charm remains a fascinating and intriguing artifact with a rich history and cultural significance.

The Egg is a symbol of both wealth and health. During Easter celebrations, it is customary for the matriarch of the family to bake a traditional sweet bread known as "folar," which contains a whole egg (sometimes more than one) inside the loaf. It is believed that whoever is lucky enough to get the egg will be blessed with good luck for the rest of the year. This tradition has been passed down for generations and continues to be an important part of Portuguese culture today.

Cartas Da Tocar is a type of prayer written on a piece of paper for healing purposes. It is often placed on the body of the afflicted and carried around for good luck and times of need. The paper is consecrated by a priest. When one touches the paper, they should recite the following words, which should be memorized: "Jesus entered, was victorious and mocked, and had all he wished, may I have from NN all I may wish." To perform the ritual, one should first say three Christmas masses over the paper and place them under the altar stone. Then, the paper should be placed in a butcher shop for one night, in the stair of justice (possibly gallows) for another night, and by the sea for a third night. Finally, three Gospels of St. John should be recited with an invested priest. This information comes from the Lisbon Inquisitors notebooks and was translated by Jose Leitao.

Cubrant

The belief in the evil eye, also known as the Jealous eye, is prevalent in many cultures around the world. In the Azores, Cubrant is the term used to describe this malevolent power that can bring misfortune, ill health, and bad luck to those who are unfortunate enough to be on its receiving end. It is believed that all it takes is a mere look of jealousy from someone who wishes you harm to activate the evil eye. The effects of the evil eye can be far-reaching, affecting everything from crops and business ventures to relationships and personal well-being. It is said that the evil eye can even sour milk and bring about disease, causing all sorts of problems in a household.

The power of the evil eye is said to be strongest when the person who sent it is jealous of something specific. For instance, if someone is envious of your loving and affectionate partner, you may find that your partner suddenly falls ill or experiences some form of bad luck, making them less affectionate than before. Children and babies are considered to be the most vulnerable to the evil eye. As beings who are fresh from Heaven and as innocent as life can be, they are more open to the energies of this new world. Pregnant mothers and babies are often protected with the use of herbs and amulets to ward off the effects of the evil eye. It is important to note that Cubrant is a type of Malefica, which has a negative connotation and is known as harmful magic. The belief in the evil eye and its impact on people's lives is deeply ingrained in many cultures, and the use of protective measures is still prevalent today.

The Rooster of Barcelos is a popular symbol of good luck and protection in many homes in the Azores and Portugal. According to the story, a poor pilgrim was wrongly accused of a crime and sentenced to death. As he was about to be executed, he made a final appeal to the judge, claiming that the rooster on the judge's plate would crow to prove his innocence. To everyone's surprise, the rooster did indeed crow, and the pilgrim was set free. Since then, heavy iron rooster statues were traditionally placed in homes for protection, as iron was believed to have protective properties. Iron production was once common in the Azores, but nowadays, the roosters are made of ceramic or metal. The imagery of the rooster can be found on tablecloths and other items, serving as a good luck charm to protect the home and its inhabitants. The Rooster of Barcelos has become a symbol of justice, honesty, and good fortune, and it is a beloved part of Portuguese folklore.

The Iron Cauldron has played an important role in the culinary culture of the Azores islands. It was widely used as a traditional cooking and scalding pot, but nowadays, it is less frequently seen around the islands. The cauldron was favored for its durability and was used for cooking and making decoctions. The Azores was renowned for its expertise in crafting cast iron cauldrons, and old postcards often depicted the cauldron, highlighting its significance in the region. Interestingly, iron is believed to have the power to deter the Moura, a mythological creature in Portuguese folklore. Despite its dwindling use, the Iron Cauldron remains a symbol of the Azores' rich cultural heritage.

Holy Water is a sacred element in many religions and is believed to have divine powers. This blessed water is often used for spiritual and physical healing. My grandmother was a firm believer in the power of holy water and had a special reverence for water from the Town of Fatima in Mainland Portugal and Our Lady of Lourdes in France. These two places are known for their miraculous apparitions of the Virgin Mary witnessed by children. According to my grandmother, the children were in a liminal space of existence and were capable of gazing upon the Lady Fatima before entering adulthood. My grandmother always kept holy water in her home and used it to bless and protect people and areas. She would add a few drops of holy water to bathwater to bless and protect the person bathing. Similarly, she would use fresh rosemary or bay to dip into the holy water and sprinkle it around an area to bless and protect that area of the home. Sometimes, my grandmother would surprise people by splashing holy water on them if she felt they needed it. However, she would never do it when she was angry, as she believed it would not work. As a result, it was not uncommon to wake up in the morning to a surprise dousing of holy water when living with her, though it could happen at any time of the day.

Fountain of the Dove

In the enchanting Mata da Serreta forest, you will come across a mystical fountain known as the "Fountain of the Dove". It is said that this fountain has magical powers to grant wishes. When you visit the fountain, you simply need to tell it what you desire and make a wish. It is believed that your wish will come true in times of dire need, especially when you have exhausted all other avenues. However, it is customary to offer something in return, akin to making a promise to fulfill your wish. These "fairy" fountains are scattered throughout the islands and their origins remain shrouded in mystery. Furthermore, Mata da Serreta is also a significant location for the Feast of Our Lady of Miracles, where the dove holds a crucial position in the cult of the Holy Spirit. If you plan to visit the island, don't miss the chance to explore this magical forest and witness its wonders for yourself.

The term "Moura" is a Portuguese word that roughly translates to "Faery," but the true meaning of the word has evolved over the past century due to popular culture such as Disney movies and fairy tales. In the past, the Moura were known as guardians of the forests and flowing water, and their stories have not been forgotten in certain areas. For instance, if you ask about the origin of the fountain in Mata Da Serreta, locals will tell you that it was put there by the Moura. The fountain is hundreds of years old and was moved many years ago, but no one knows where it originally came from or how it ended up there. The "Fountain of the Dove" is an appropriate name for this holy fountain, as doves are sacred to the goddess Astarte and a crucial symbol in the veneration of the Holy Spirit within the Cult of the Holy Spirit on the Azores Islands. The fountain's mysterious origins only add to its allure and intrigue.

If you are ever in Jardim Duque da Terceira, don't forget to visit the Old Courtyard of the Jesuit college and the Convent of Sao Francisco. The garden is home to an interesting fountain structure, which features (what appears to be) the Goddess Astarte with water flowing from her breasts into a basin below. This fountain is said to have the power to help with problems in one's love life, so it's definitely worth a visit if you're looking for a little guidance. The fountain also features an "indo american" statue blowing water out of a flute. Interestingly, this water was traditionally used to irrigate the garden, but there may be a hidden meaning behind it as well. The fountains in Mata Da Serreta and Jardim Duque Da Terceira share the same age and style. Both feature what is said to be "Indo-American Statuary" - likely a Brazilian influence, but with a distinctly Arabesque style. It's definitely a unique and beautiful sight to see.

Olive oil is a versatile cooking ingredient that has been used in the Azores for centuries. However, it's not just used for food. Many people believe that olive oil has spiritual properties that can bless a person and their home with peace. As a result, it's a common household item that is always within reach.

Fava beans have been used for their magical properties for centuries. In the Azores, these beans are believed to have protective qualities that can keep a person invisible when applied to the right spells. The locals also bless these beans and add them to charm bags as a divinatory tool. The Book of Saint Cyprian and Sorceress of Angra are two sources that mention the use of Fava beans in magical practices. Apart from their magical properties, Fava beans are also a popular food in many parts of the world. They are a great source of protein, fiber, and other essential nutrients. In fact, some cultures have been cultivating and consuming Fava beans for thousands of years.

The book of St. Cyprian is a fascinating but controversial book of magic that has sparked fear and intrigue over the years. It is a classic book that documents Iberian Folk magic and contains a wealth of information on various magical practices, including spells, rituals, and incantations. While some have criticized it as a book of Christian propaganda, it is still widely regarded as an important historical text that sheds light on the magical practices of the past. One of the most intriguing stories in the book of St. Cyprian is that of Justina, a beautiful maiden who was the target of Aglaias, a man who desired her more than anything to be his wife. However, Justina did not reciprocate his feelings, and after an attempted kidnapping, Aglaias sought out the help of the famous sorcerer Cyprian to bring Justina to her knees in adulation of him. Cyprian, being a skilled magician, sent a Demon of Fornication to Justina, hoping to bend her to Aglaias's will. However, Justina's unwavering faith in prayer and her belief in the power of God thwarted the demon's advances. After putting the fear of God into the demon, it went back to Cyprian to tell of its defeat. Determined to achieve his goal, Cyprian then sent two stronger demons to Justina in the night, and eventually, even the Devil himself came to witness her power. However, her wit and prayer instilled fear in these demons, and they too were unable to sway her. Despite his failure to seduce Justina, Cyprian continued to harbor feelings of shame and rage towards her. He sent plagues and evil entities to her home, hoping to break her spirit. However, Justina continued to pray, and all of the plagues were cured, and the evil dissipated. Cyprian was ridiculed and mocked for his inability to seduce a pious girl, and he soon realized the power of prayer and its ability to deflect demonic forces from their intended target. Inspired by Justina's unwavering faith, Cyprian joined the Christian Church and soon rose in its ranks. He learned that by denouncing the power of the Devil and making the sign of the cross, he could send the Devil packing. The book of St. Cyprian is a testament to the power of prayer and faith in God, and it has inspired countless people over the years to turn to prayer and spirituality as a means of protection against the forces of darkness.

The book of Saint Cyprian is also a significant source of information on Azorean folk practices. However, it can be seen as Catholic propaganda, as Saint

Cyprian was a well-known practicing sorcerer who found the Christian God to be the most powerful. He converted to Christianity and became a bishop. It is worth noting that dedicating yourself to a jealous and vengeful God can help focus your power. However, many of the spells mentioned in the book of Saint Cyprian can be disturbing and should not be attempted unless you feel confident in doing so. Furthermore, it is important to adjust them to not entertain cruelty and domination.

In the Catholic religion, the saints hold a significant place in the hearts of the faithful. They are revered and venerated for their holiness and are often called upon to intercede with God on behalf of those in need. Saints are believed to have the power to work miracles and help believers achieve their desired results. Similar to the deities of old, saints serve as a source of inspiration and guidance to those who seek their aid. Through prayer and devotion, Catholics seek to establish a closer relationship with the saints and gain their blessings. The tradition of saint worship has been a central part of the Catholic faith for centuries.

The Beguines.

The history of the Beguines within the Azores is a fascinating tale that provides insight into the lives of religious women in the Middle Ages. The Beguines were a group of lay religious women originally from Flanders (Belgium) who worked in fiber art, including harvesting, weaving, and dying wool to be made into garments like the capelo o capote that was worn by the women, but was also sold to generate income from their "convent". The Capelo, a traditional Azorean robe, is said to come from them specifically. However, the Beguines were not just skilled artisans, they were also known for their commitment to caring for the poor and the sick. They used their knowledge of herbs and prayer to heal the sick and help those in need. It is believed that they fled to the Azores to reduce suspicion under the eye of inquisitors. Though they did not necessarily practice witchcraft as we think of it today, they were in charge of taking care of the poor, and their work with herbs and prayer made them fall under scrutiny of the Catholic Church. Despite this, the Beguines remained faithful to Christ on their own terms, committing themselves to a simple life of helping the poor and healing the sick. They were a valuable resource to the Azorean people as they valued education and independence for women, and many of them could read and write. They brought much of their healing knowledge through the use of herbs and prayer to the Azores and beyond, leaving behind a legacy that continues to inspire people to this day. One of the most significant contributions that the Beguines made to the Azorean culture was the Festival of the Holy Spirit. This festival is celebrated annually and is an important part of Azorean culture. The Beguines are credited with bringing this festival to the Azores, and it is a testament to their enduring legacy. The Festival of the Holy Spirit is a time for people to come together, share food and drink, and celebrate their faith. It is a time to remember and honor the contributions of the Beguines to the Azorean culture and to celebrate the enduring legacy they have left behind.

Menstruation In Portugal is a taboo subject. For the Yearly Pig Killing or A Matança do Porco, Women are generally forbidden to touch the Pig, the Pork, or the Sausage (and in this case, also abstain from sex)— the story of why this varies from region to region. In the Book "Blood Magic" It is said that the Pork and Penis can be spoiled if a menstruating woman touches it. But in my own Azorean Community, I have asked about why a menstruating woman would be excluded from the annual pig killing, and it has been said that if a woman is menstruating, it is due to her needing to rest instead of needing to work. So this could be a more modern interpretation or not. A Euphemism for menstruation in the Azores is "Tia Maria" Comes to visit.

Laying of Hands:

The practice of laying hands to remove negative energies from the body is an ancient tradition that has been passed down through generations. It involves giving a brisk massage, sometimes with pounding on the back and/or sweeping out mists of stagnant energy that come up off the body, while reciting prayers to release these entities. In some cases, negative energies need to be transmuted by taking them into oneself and releasing them through belching or blowing quick breaths. I have a personal connection to this practice, as my grandmother was a deeply spiritual woman who could pray for hours and days on end. When I was a child, I underwent surgery on one of my eyes to correct amblyopia. While recovering in the hospital, my grandmother prayed by my bedside, and I soon began to cry tears of blood. She believed this was a sign of a miraculous healing, and indeed, the surgery was ultimately successful, giving me 20/20 vision well into my 30s. Looking back, I realize that being born with such an ailment likely meant that I had been affected by the evil eye as a developing fetus. Fortunately, I had access to a range of healing opportunities through my family and skilled surgeons in the area, which helped me overcome this challenge and live a healthy, fulfilling life, thanks to Grandma.

Seeking Voices: The divination practice of "Seeking Voices" described by Jose Leitao in his book "Seeking Voices and Finding Meaning: Portuguese Verbal Divination" is a fascinating process used in the Azores, particularly on the island of Sao Miguel. This practice is often used to obtain information about who someone will marry. During the practice, a group of people walk in a procession to a holy place, praying the rosary or silently counting their beads. As they walk, they listen carefully to the words they hear coming from houses and on the street. Once they return, they combine the words they heard and interpret them to arrive at an answer or advice.

In the Azores, there are some interesting beliefs about witches and their signs.

For instance, it is believed that if someone can put their hand in a boiling pot of water without burning themselves, they might be a witch. However, it's also said that this ability can be achieved through years of practice and cooking soups and other hot items. Another belief is that when a woman lets their hair down they become more powerful and can practice all sorts of witchcraft. (women typically had kept their hair in a kerchief) It's also said that exposing one's breasts during a ritual act can make the act more powerful. Interestingly, being the seventh-born child is also considered a sign of potential magic and witchcraft. However, it's important to note that this doesn't necessarily mean the child will become a witch; they could also become a werewolf in the future.

THE PORTUGUESE INQUISITION

Depiction of the "carocha" hat

During the Portuguese Inquisition, which spanned from the late 15th to the late 18th centuries, many people were accused of various crimes such as Witchcraft, Sorcery, Superstitions, Divination, Healing, and Revelations among other things. The Inquisition was a time of fear and paranoia, and many innocent people were persecuted and punished for these so-called crimes. The Azores Islands, isolated in the Atlantic Ocean, were not immune to the reach of the Inquisition. Many people on these islands were accused of crimes and faced severe punishments such as imprisonment, torture, and even death. The Inquisitors were ruthless in their pursuit of suspected heretics, and many people lived in constant fear of being accused and punished. Despite the harsh treatment that many people faced, their names still live on today and serve as a reminder of the injustices that were carried out during the Inquisition. Each name tells the story of a person who had dreams and sought to survive the best they could in this world. Their lives were cut short by the ruthless actions of the Inquisitors, but their memory lives on. For those interested in learning more about the Inquisition and its impact on the Azores Islands, there are many resources available. The antt.dglab.gov.pt website is a great place to start, as it includes photocopies of the original inquisitor's notes in Portuguese. These documents provide a window into the past and allow us to better understand the lives of those who lived during this dark time in history.

This is the story of Barbara de Figueiredo

"In 1652, a priest named Gaspar Cardoso accused two women of sorcery. These women were Barbara de Figueiredo and her niece, Maria da Fé, who, according to Gaspar, had bewitched his brother, the priest João Cardoso. Gaspar's accusation sparked an investigation into the matter, and a series of testimonies were collected from witnesses who had seen or heard of Barbara's sorcery.

It was known for a few years that João was not really faithful to his vows, and he had an ardent 'illicit friendship' with Barbara. However, as his professional responsibilities grew, he found himself unable to spend as much time with Barbara as she wished, and he grew increasingly bored with her to the point of breaking off their relationship.

Barbara had apparently taken this very personally and, being a famed sorceress in Angra, proceeded to cast all sorts of malefica on João, who had, in the meantime, gone mad. Gaspar had tried to remedy this situation, even agreeing to pay Barbara a hefty amount so that she would remove her sorceries, but to no avail. Being now desperate, Gaspar was denouncing her, offering, besides his testimony, a list of names who could be questioned and who would corroborate his statements. The investigation into the matter was thorough, and several witnesses were summoned to give their testimonies.

Isabel da Costa, who had lived with Barbara for an extended period of time when she came to Angra from the island of Pico, confirmed the story. João Cardoso was in a carnal relationship with Barbara and ended up leaving her. Barbara attempted many times to get him back, but to no avail.

The last and most dramatic of these was when she decided to go on a pilgrimage to São Mateus where João was serving as a priest. There João once again rejected her, and, coming out of the church in a fury, Barbara went straight to the beach, where she collected a few small rocks, moss, and driftwood. Taking all of these things to a friend's house, Barbara made a small pile with the rocks, stuffed the wood in the center of this, placed a pot with water and the moss over everything, and lit the wood so it would boil. At that time, Isabel didn't hear what Barbara was saying while she was doing this, but she did see that, after she was done, she went back to the beach and threw a vintem (a coin) into the ocean (although another witness says she did this when she collected the ingredients). From here on, Barbara would be frequently seen doing all sorts of different rituals.

Once, she was seen with her hair down and uncombed, with a three-legged bench upside down in front of her, two lamps, and an image of Saint Erasmus. Other times she was spinning some tow while saying: "I do not spin a string of tow, but the heart of João Cardoso, which I have in my hand." After which she would tie several knots in this string and throw them behind her back with the help of her niece, burning them afterward.

Isabel had also seen a needle Barbara had, which had been used to sew the shroud of a dead man, with which she would make stitches in a person's clothes to either harm them or have them under her control, saying words such as: "I sew thee with the needle of a dead man, so as thou may be mad for me, and only these words hear." Other words she heard were: "The Devil entered the River Jordan so as to speak, and nine rods of juniper bring, and in the millstone of Barabbas and Satanas sharpen them and in the heart of João Cardoso carve them, so as he may not be, nor wait, nor eat, nor drink until he speaks to me."

Other times Barbara had mentioned that the seed of a man, taken after sex, should be put into a glass of wine and given back to him to drink, and this would make him agreeable.

Another witness, Francisco Luís, a carpenter, mentioned that Barbara had quite a fame for being a sorceress, and she even had some magical fava beans which were worked with by putting some of these beans inside the severed head of a black cat and then burying it.

Maria Alves, another witness, mentioned that Barbara was also known for doing coscinomancy (sieve divination), in the name of 'Saint Peter, Saint Paul, Saint Pelourinho, and Saint Pelonario', as well as a devotion she did lying down with her hand and legs crossed while prayed to Our Lady of Encarnacion.

Most witnesses offered very consistent stories, and, overall, Barbara was a famous woman, not only due to her sorcerous inclinations but also because she was known for her healings.

In particular, there were stories of her curing a nasty cut a man had on his foot, from the blow of an ax, which she sewed shut while praying. But, without a doubt, she was most famous for having, allegedly, killed several people with her sorceries. All of these testimonies, being collected, were sent to Lisbon, where they were copied and analyzed.

The case didn't seem to spur too much interest in the Inquisition, as only in 1659 did they order an investigation. This was once again performed in Angra, where all the original witnesses were summoned to repeat their testimonies from seven years before.

All of them confirmed their previous testimonies, with the only change being that, apparently, by now Barbara had married and was living on Rua De Galo in Angra.

The story of Barbara de Figueiredo and her niece, Maria da Fé, is a fascinating tale of love, jealousy, and sorcery in 17th-century Angra. It is the story of a woman who gained fame for her sorcery but was ultimately undone by her jealousy and desire for revenge. Despite her reputation for being a sorceress, she was also known for her healings, which added to her notoriety. Her story sheds light on the power of jealousy and the dangers of getting sexually involved with priests, and it is a reminder of the role of the Inquisition in investigating such cases.

The Church of São Mateus where João served as a Priest.

Here are more people accused of various crimes prosecuted during the Portugues inquisition:

António de Gouveia, a 29-year-old man from Praia, Terceira, Azores was accused of practicing curandera/healing, superstitions, and witchcraft. He was sentenced to an auto-da-fé on July 14, 1561, for heresy.

As part of his sentence, he had to publicly renounce his beliefs with his head uncovered and a lit candle in his hand. He was detained in prison and suspended from his orders and priestly office indefinitely, preventing him from curing or using his office again.

However, he managed to flee from the prison of Colégio da Doctrina on May 2, 1564, but was later arrested and sentenced again on September 29, 1564, to exile on the galleys (slavery). Due to an illness caused by the sun, he escaped again and traveled through Italy, France, and Germany. Upon his request, the penalty of the galleys was lifted, and he was released from them. He was allowed to go back to Terceira Island on November 18, 1566, but was forbidden from returning to Lisbon. As he did not comply with the sentence, he was sent back to prison on August 26, 1567, and was sentenced to two years of exile in Brazil and banned from entering Lisbon again. On October 9, 1571, he was once again imprisoned in the Santo Ofício of Lisbon, chained in irons on a ship from Pernambuco, Brazil. There were serious accusations against him at the Inquisition table.

Mariana da Coluna was a 22-year-old nun from São Miguel who was accused of sorcery in 1633 and 1637 AD.

Jerónima de Sousa was a 70-year-old woman from Sao Miguel who was arrested in Ponta Delgada between 1619 to 1621. She was accused of witchcraft and sorcery. As a punishment, she was required to attend a public ritual of penance called the "auto-da-fe". During the ritual, she had to hold a candle in her hand and wear a carocha on her head. She was also required to make a slight abjuration, serve an exile of three years in Brazil, receive instruction in the Catholic faith, perform spiritual penances and pay the costs of her punishment.

The accused **Francisco** was a black slave who was accused of sorcery in Angra, Terceira in 1743. It was rumored that he was the child of Agostinho Zimbrão Borges..

Inês Francisca da Costa, from Franca do Campo on the island of São Miguel, was accused of witchcraft and sorcery.

Padre Francisco de Santa Rosa was a 28-year-old priest who died while in prison in 1761-1762. He was accused of witchcraft and superstitious activity, and apparently died of natural causes while under trial. He was a priest of the Order of Sao Francisco on Pico Island.

CATARINA BERNARDA DO SACRAMENTO was accused of Witchcraft and Sorcery in 1792. It is unclear what happened to her afterwards.

Amaro Fernandes, a 50-year-old farmer from Agualva, Terceira Island, was accused of divination, cures, and other revelations in 1659. He was sentenced in 1660 to public humiliation, auto-da-fe, exile to Brazil for 5 years, and repayment of costs.

Mateus Vaz, a 25-year-old man from Praia, Graciosa Island, was accused of superstitions and witchcraft during the years 1711-1716. As a result, he was sentenced to an Auto-de-fe, which included the confiscation of his property, abjuration, imprisonment, perpetual penitential habit, public flogging, banishment for five years to the galleys, and spiritual penances.

Baltasar Gonçalves, a 50-year-old blacksmith from Angra, Terceira Island, was accused of having visions and revelations in 1583-1584. He was eventually declared insane and released to his island.

Bárbara da Conceição was accused of superstitions and sorcery in 1742-1743 on Sao Miguel Island. She died in prison in 1743.

Francisca de Oliveira, a woman from Sao Miguel, was accused of practicing superstitions and sorcery between 1792-1794.

Aurélia Feliciana was a skilled weaver hailing from Terceira island. However, her life took a tragic turn when she was accused of sorcery, which led to a private auto-da-fe on November 24th, 1792. The verdict resulted in her being admitted to the Hospital Real de S. José, where she was diagnosed with madness by the medical professors. It's a heartbreaking story of a talented individual whose life was destroyed due to unfounded accusations and superstitions.

Sebastião was a 20-year-old who was born as a slave. He hailed from Graciosa Island and was accused of sorcery. He served as a slave of Captain João Neto da Cunha, and in 1692, he was sentenced for his alleged crime of sorcery. The penalty he received was a controlled beating in the streets, which was not meant to draw blood or lead to his death. The inquisitors had the discretion to imprison him and provide schooling on Catholicism. He was also banished for three years to the Castle of Castro Marim as a form of penitence. In addition to this, he was also required to pay all the costs associated with his punishment.

Padre Frei Francisco do Rosário was a 50-year-old priest who was accused of blasphemy during his stay in Praia da Vitória, ilha Terceira, although he was originally from Brazil. His sentence was an auto-da-fe on 09/16/1781. He was required to abjure and was deprived of an active and passive voice, as well as the exercise of his orders for five years. Following this, he was exiled to Cape Verde for another five years. After his initial exile, he was sent to the Lisbon prisons, and then once again, he was exiled to the most remote convent in his province, where he would stay. He spent one year in prison in the same convent where the sentence was read on a festa day, by a notary of the Holy Office. Spiritual penalties, penances, and ordinary instruction were imposed on him as well.

In 1637, a woman named **Beatriz Dos Santos**, also known as Beatriz Rodrigues from the island of Sao Miguel, was accused of sorcery. She was arrested and given instructions on the Catholic Faith, along with spiritual penances. Additionally, she was flogged in the public streets of Lisbon "Citra Sanguinis Efesionem" and exiled to the Island of Principe for ten years.

In 1731, a man named **Manuel Correia**, aged 40 and from Sao Miguel, was accused of sorcery and labeled as a "poor man" and a "beggar". As per his sentence, he was required to receive instruction in the Catholic Faith, and was then dragged through the streets with the label of "sorcerer". He was further humiliated and robbed of his dignity by being exiled and forbidden from entering Eastern and Western Lisbon.

In the year 1620, **Susana Jorge**, who was from Sao Miguel and aged between 35 to 40 years old, was accused of witchcraft and sorcery. She was sentenced to be publicly whipped, given "spiritual penances," and exiled to Brazil for ten years with the obligation to repay the costs.

In 1793 two women named **Maria do Rosário and Ana Joaquina** were accused of superstitious behaviors. The details of their alleged actions are unknown, but it is a reminder of the historical persecution and oppression of those who were seen as different or practicing beliefs outside of the norm.

Depiction of an "auto-da-fe" in Lisbon

Further Reading:

"Flora of the Azores" A field Guide by Hanno Schafer

Facebook group: "Azorean Herbalism" : https://www.facebook.com/groups/329838218011203

http://digitarq.arquivos.pt/details?id=2314037

https://repositorio.uac.pt/handle/10400.3/1677

https://www.research.ed.ac.uk/portal/files/9338068/DESIGNING_FOOD_CULTURES.pdf

https://www.ncbi.nlm.nih.gov/pmc/

articles/PMC6724175/

https://
www.mdpi.com/1660-3397/16/8/248

https://www.gutenberg.org/
files/32528/32528-h/32528-h.htm

Diabruras, Santidades e Profecias(1894:
111) by Teixeira da Aragão

Bibliotheca Valenciana
Book of Saint Cyprian José Leitão

"New unknown Archaeological Data in
Azores: The Hipogea of the Brazil Mount,
Terceira Island, Portugal" ~ Anabela
Joaquinito

Stucky, J. Tanit of Carthage 2009 Lammas
Vol 8-4

Antt.dglab.gov.pt

"Blood Magic; The Anthropology of
Menstruation" by Buckley and Gottlieb

https://pt.azoresguide.net/dia-do-

trabalhador-a-tradicao-dos-maios-nos-acores/?
fbclid=IwAR1cvcVXdQtJQ4aUo38X9FljOfI
pORNktkMNoiAtQgBQKW_8vw8iKxTYeU
Y

https://
herminiusmons.wordpress.com/2018/06/
24/ataegina/

https://www.jstor.org/stable/30035123